LEARNING THE WAY

Winner of the United States Award

of the International Poetry Forum

1967

LEARNING
THE WAY

James Den Boer

University of Pittsburgh Press

Copyright © 1968 by the University of Pittsburgh Press
Library of Congress Catalog Card Number 68-12733
Manufactured in the United States of America

Some of the poems in this volume first appeared in *Northwest Review*, *The Mad River Review*, *The Southern Poetry Review*, *Jeopardy*, *The Colorado Quarterly*, *Poetry Northwest*, *The North American Review*, *Colorado State Review*, *The Fiddlehead*, and *The Washingtonian*.

The International Poetry Forum and the University of Pittsburgh Press acknowledge with gratitude the assistance of the Junior League of Pittsburgh, Inc., in making this book possible.

To Daphne, who knows

Contents

III

I

Learning the Way

§ Each winter, after the first snow,
we began our game of tracking
on the bluffs above Lake Michigan.

I read in summer on the tricks
of Indians, and practiced them on winter
friends a long half hour behind;

learned to leap from grass clump
to stone, find hard ways to go
over the frozen fields. Alone

before the rest, with the slow boom
of waves against the packed ice
cracking below, I tested the limits

of my cunning in isolation.
Long winds from the plains tuned
the steps of these wilderness dances.

Diving for Snapper

§ At dusk, after working
all day in the sun,
we come through light mist
on the river past
quiet birds. On
the water waterbeetles spin

in perfect circles. In old
swimming trunks, each
with just a knife,
my friend and I jump cold
into the brown water,
duck heads once, then push

through junk along the bank,
wading in mud until
it's deep enough to swim.
We call it turtling.
To keep near we stroke
out side-by-side.

Here, he says, look, take
your knife, watch what
I do, this first time.
The wide river beneath
my chin, I know
what is below, pull air

into my lungs as he dives,
his feet suddenly
kicking for the bottom.
I float on top, my eyes
open just under water
as he goes down for snapper.

I see him close on one,
near the bottom where
it lives, beak open
and browsing. This is what
we go down for, what we dare,
the pair of us against

turtles—he kicks toward
it from behind, grips
the long neck hard
with one gloved hand;
then up, eyes blind with water
to explain "turtle"

with his knife,
slashing hard once.
Blood spreads on water
as the turtle thrashes
at arm's length. So, we begin
with knives to bring them in.

Jennett's Sedge

§ Local boys in summer after bass
are the only ones who dare
wander off the nature trail
into that dark tangle
of creeper and low pine.

This Is Diamondback Country,
said a sign, Remember
You Are Visitors Here.

Moving warily from sign
to sign, a visitor's eye on
everything, we see a terrapin,
here in Jennett's Sedge,
in from Diamond Shoals.

The final bend of the trail
opens to a warm sun-dry
hollow where snakes like to lie;
one did, then pulled its markings
with it into the black water.

The Park Service reassures
us from the nearest post
with Latin names
for oak, yaupon, wild grape.

From the North Northeast

§ The weather held all that week,
from the north northeast,
the rain full of salt,
the wind steady, not cold,
the daily grays and whites
in their way more colorful
than the small dry flowers
of purple and white

in the ditches along the road.
The tall lunar fleshed weeds
cupped their seeds among
guarding thistles. At the edge
of the surf the whip
of the wind would knock
you down; we held each other
against it, the breathing

of such a beast, at land's
end. Here in the wind,
we forgot the great cities,
the streets and neon found
inland, west and north,
of this casual finger,
Hatteras Island. Then the lee
of the dunes was so sudden

a relief that, staggering, we
still feared the sound,
that it would leap again over
the red thin slatted fencing
and the rows of sown dune grass.
Above, the silent clouds flow
darkly through rare dark distances:
this weather will not pass.

After Shark at Hatteras

§ We slit the belly of the ray
and scrape the guts out with a knife:
this is the way you get bait
for shark. The stripped intestines
gleam with color on the sand
as we chop them into pieces,
hook-size, and hook them twice.

The ray we bury in a shallow
grave, just above the waves'
reach and wash. Its tail sticks
up an inch or two to show us where.
The mess of guts goes in a pail
and I push my hands in to feel
whatever life is left there.

A harsh day—the surf crashing
like stones around our legs,
and out in the dark currents,
running back and forth, the fins
of shark and then their heavy backs
cut and heave through chop.
We cast and stumble on the shore.

Our hands freeze and ache with salt
in the small cuts from hook,
knife, and grass. The shark
are far beyond us, and our reach,
cruising on their own long
round and cast for food.
We reel in, then, and throw the pail

of ray guts in the surf—the day
ends in our defeat; the implacable
dark-finned shark outlast us,
searching beyond breakers, where water
backs against the bar and fills
with food. Our prints fill, on the
shore, as we head back of dunes.
So much we need does not need us.

Thoughts of the Sea in the City

§ In this metal city,
my metal head
reverberating
to air hammer,
sirens, hustle,

glass and brick
falling from old
buildings,
I force my mind
to the sea,

its roll and chop,
the sand beaches
spit from Nags Head
out past
Teach's waters.

Here buccaneers
of truck and hack
go overboard.
Waves of heat
make me sick;

I shiver, see
the virus-laden
birds wheel
the bright towers
for potato chips,

tinfoil.
I too whirl here.
The gulls
at Hatteras scream
from the rocks

to their feast,
the flesh of cut bait.
We throw
long lines out
in dark surf.

On Isle Royale

1. *The First Day In*

The rocks give up to sun
lichen gray, lime green,
white, bright orange, black;

we crush through with boots,
getting color photographs.
Back from shore dark trees

cage the hidden moose and wolf
together in the northern nights.
Loon screams to loon.

Pike sulk and mosey in the weeds
ringing the inland ponds.
We kneel to worship mushrooms,

dead-white Indian pipe;
strip blueberries into our hats, then
sleep like logs near logs.

2. *The Small Lakes*

The small lakes of the north
look up forever to the skies,
the forest whispers: look there,
look there. The sky drifts.

When the voices of the pines,
maple, oak and birch speak,
we feel the pressure
in our blood. The lakes see.

The clouds blow over,
listening to the birds,
the forest flowers: Indian pipe,
bunchberry, hepatica. The forest speaks.

Clouds feel the beat of veins,
the whisper of blood coursing,
drawn to the lakes; we speak
to the trees: here, here.

3. *Sea Blood Lakes Eyes*

The seas are continuous
and salt as blood, making no
distinctions possible (drawing

from a vein in the crook
of the elbow is the same
as drawing from the blue vein

that lies across the bone
of the ankle); the definition
of fresh water is in

its disjunction, the diversity
of that which ponds or lakes,
as eyes, see (light drawn

from quartz in stone,
the sheen of wet hair
on deer or beaver,

dark leaves shining underfoot,
light seen differently as
every dream), deep and clear.

4. *The Fallen Birch*

I balanced to the top
of the fallen birch
to angle for long pike,

edging out from the rotting
bank, no anchor for roots

cut under by water.
Deep in branches, I cast
straight up and out,

waited for the slow
pull against my reeling.

Pack-rod guides glinted
like small suns in the leaves.
Between earth and water,

I had angled to this end,
vain for reach to deep water,
beyond shore-strength,

and now was caught, branched
and yearning, baited,

when the fish bumped bumped
then hit, and I set it hard
from the weakness

of my position. Leaves shivered
bright side up around

my face, water fed beneath me
at the shore, as I hauled
against the reluctant muscle

of the single-minded,
deeply-committed, artless pike.

5. *The Land Asks*

What's in you? the best land asks,
insists there is an answer,

that you know it, and encourages
best answers. I am well-prepared:

good boots, good pack, good hat.
There are things I fear

that do not stop me
from going on. I remember

what is best remembered,
forgive myself for what I must

forget. The cow moose and calf
browse down the meadow to the water,

the loon stays under until
her cry has died across the lake,

wolf tracks shine near
the fish-cleaning stump at dawn.

I give my best answer:
nothing between me and what is.

In Woods, in Meadows

§ She asked to use my sleeping bag,
took my poncho for a ground-cloth,
and left for meadows beyond
the stand of birches and red pine,
leaving for the night.
I walked with her to the edge.

"My mother told me to sleep
in meadows; if I did—well,
there are fewer hard roots
in good meadows, and fewer noises.
My mother said that grasses
are a bed for young girls,
with hair like new hay and faces
like fields, open and black-eyed."

"I know your mother," I said.
"She is dark as a wood. When the trees
begin to answer, talking in your sleep,
that's when calmness beyond
the calmness of girls does some good.
No one weeps in meadows,
or grows up. My sleeping bag
has never been in meadows, won't
do you any good. Why didn't
your father tell you where to sleep?"

"My father doesn't sleep well,"
she said, "because my mother is a wood.
There are some things I don't want

to know. Everything is hard in woods.
Things come too close. In meadows
you can see far and be seen,
you have some chance, some choices.
When mothers are a wood, they teach
daughters meadows, for their good."

"In meadows you sleep with both eyes shut,"
I said. "In woods one's open, watching out.
You have to care where you are.
Young girls are much safer in woods,
because they're more afraid.
My sleeping bag was never meant for two.
Meadows are too good, woods true.
Life's difficult. That's what woods teach."

"My mother is dark as woods,
but she sleeps well beside my father,
as he stirs," she said. "I want
to sleep in meadows so that he
can sleep. Let bright meadows
do our watching for us, so our eyes
can shut. I want to sleep where light
from moon and stars can reach.
I can't reach you in the dark."

I have chosen dark before for others'
sake, and left her at the edge,
where woods and meadows meet and touch.

Owned Land

for Catherine Bateson

§ Driving through rain,
north from Pittsfield,
we talked of Israel,
where stones are Arabs

on the ancient fields.
Here fence-posts
are the only Indians left,
edging the hard farms,

dreaming the seasons.
Well-known as hands,
this land was bought from spirits.
Religion chants

from the turned stones,
the turned fields.
The Algonquin prays in Hebrew
kneeling by the barn.

The Red Salamander

§ The red salamander on the road
has two small black spots on its neck,
ringed with yellow;

its spine is gooseflesh,
but it is still in my hand.
My thumb warms, calms.

Logging trucks, rigged
high with hardwood down from the mountains,
backfire in low gear

past us kneeling in gravel
on the narrow shoulders, bark and chips
trailing their storm.

Caught here, we can only
be still: my thumb like a log against
its spine, the storm of my breathing.

The Frog

§ On the dark road
the belly of the dead frog
glowed like a stone;

always reaching
for things to throw to keep
things back,

I touched the white stone
and was thrown back.
My fingers glowed

but left dark prints
where I took flesh
for stone.

Stones

§ Along the climbing road
the stones are chipped,
sharp, click late at night

under stars drawing
stone's heat. Last week
we gathered from the beach

stones tumbled smooth,
round, all the whites,
the grays, the browns.

If, up from the sea
to the mountains
stones differ from

caress to cut,
then I would take two stones
with me with you.

The Pheasant

for Megali, at four years

§ She walks out among the birds;
she calls to them in the fields back of the house,
"Here, birds, here, here!"

And the birds hear her,
for when I spread the black feathers on the head
of the cock pheasant,

bleeding in the sink, it has ears,
neat as buttonholes! She is not afraid of birds
that hear her, or that see her,

for she sees the pheasant's
eyes like black beads under the running water,
swirling away red. Birds fly,

she knows, as I cut
through the shattered bone of a wing and hook
my finger under strong muscle

and tendon. Birds eat corn,
as she does, for its gullet is packed with kernels;
I show her lungs, for breathing,

heart, and its dark intricate chambers.
With the point of my knife, I dig out birdshot,
drop one on the worn linoleum

so we can hear it hit.
She picks it up and holds it in her fist.
Salting down these wounds

to leech them dry,
I dress such innocence as I can find.
In one hand a feather,

in the other, shot,
my daughter dances in the kitchen like a savage,
for this butcher's love.

Two Grandfathers

§ 1. *Grandfather Reading*

Grandfather's fields are paved
with asphalt, he grinds his teeth
on carbon dust, and raves
against the dying of his wife

from arteriosclerosis, gas,
and diabetes; his own breath
is short. He longs for grass.
He feels, he feels his life

and hers are gently blurring
into one, and that one
life will soon be out. No hurry
to it, he whispers to his son

in greasy clothes and welding mask,
who lives in flames, almost a boss,
and breathes that gas.
Grandfather clucks to horses

who thundered in their stalls
for sixty years for him.
From her darkened room Grandmother calls
for brandy; he curses them,

the doctors, lawyers, graveyard
men, and pages over Calvin
in the Dutch. A postcard
photo of his grandson tears him

in two, until he tears all the pictures
in the house in two and falls
among the broken glass and mirrors.
Again, in Dutch, Grandmother calls.

2. *Grandfather in the Garden*

Grandfather left his straw hat on
in the sun as he napped,
stretching his six feet and odd inches
along the striped deck chair
under the backyard chestnut.
We children brought him raspberries,
staining our fingers blue,
and he ate them one by one
between snoozes.

All that summer he napped there,
while the incredible white blossoms
of the chestnut died,
and the hard nuts like a mace's
spiked head began to drop
around him. He napped and gazed,
dreaming the two black-coated
Mormons again at his door, young
men to bellow Scripture back at,
and furiously drive from the parlor.

He was dying, some cancer eating
him inside while the chestnuts browned.
All the neighborhood knew his strength,
except the usual idiot boy,
who snatched Grandfather's hat
and ran. Grandfather rising,
calling for his thick cane and God,
awoke to death with a mouthful of blood.

Father Finds a Job in America

§ Following his father, to this land and work,
my father limps through more than thirty years

at his long work; he welds himself with
hands in flames, his face dark-masked.

Noon whistles, and he eats alone each day,
chewing his loneliness for bread and meat,

brushing away flies, waxed paper at his feet.
Through the dusty windows where he stands,

ignites and melts his steel, America
stretches across its famous fields and hills

farther than his light-scarred and weakened
eyes can see. All he sees are pheasants

pecking for seeds of grasses blown down
among the rusting twisted scrap-heaps

by what he believes is wind beginning
in the sea he never saw. He enters

the heavy mask, and his children swim
up to meet him in that green sea-light;

those he fathered in this land of flames
that burn his seed to loneliness like steel.

Kitchen Hymn

§ He tried explaining to his
mother the uses of art,
"When a bird sings . . . ."
She sniffed, Dutch Cleanser
in her hand, at the sink.

They lived on Superior Avenue,
because they were; later
moved to First Street, because
they were: serious, neat,
white as Dutch Cleanser.

They led the town in scouring,
their only art; second
generation users of Dutch
Cleanser, they scraped
and scraped to break down

stains. Outside the window
above the sink, birds sang
in the plum trees;
in the cupboards, cans
of Dutch Cleanser questioned

him like deacons about
his soul: "The world is slowly
yellowing, how can you
sing?" Dutch Cleanser shakes
down on Wisconsin like snow

in the long winters, cold rinses
the elect and all others alike.
Think on Dutch Cleanser,
abrasive, hard-working,
crooning its own song in this sink.

The Uncle

§ Counting seconds between lightning
and thunder, the old man at the window
calculates his position:
how near or far he is from the storm.

He is counting many things:
the number of his years, the beat
of his heart, how many others
have died, the times love has moved

him to ask, "How near or far am I
from what is real, what is continuing?"
or, "How many heartbeats are left,
and what is it I have done?"

Six, five, four, three, two, one:
the storm is moving near, now beats
through him to the heart, answering,
"This close," and "This is what storms do."

North Pier

§ Our harbor pier dog-legged one mile out
into Lake Michigan each year I grew up

on this western shore; townspeople walked
out on Sundays after church to watch

the ore boats smoke slowly at the edge
of sight, going south to Gary and the mills.

Each winter covered it with ice, crumbling
the concrete blocks in spring; summer turned

the steel walk too hot for touch. Everyone
in town had trudged that mile out sometime

to stand below the tall red light, covering
their ears against the horn that bellowed

as the fog rolled in—a small town crying
from its furthest reach out from shore,

hoping to be heard beyond horizons beyond reach.
We called together for the fog or water

to bring in to harbor anything for answers.
Many ached for years from that two-mile walk

out and back again. Some of us answered ourselves,
walked out beyond the end, and disappeared.

On My Hands

§ They are bumpy and ridged
as Wisconsin, with tics

beneath the skin like
a cow unperching flies

up into airy circles:
small, tight and angry;

neat fields etched
in the moraine,

trout streams
and simple creeks.

Sometimes the fingers
are silos, or fly-rods,

and the veins like ropes
in the bull's nose-ring

or the lay of long mounds
where we dug clay shards

and Indian arrowheads.
The knuckles are boxcar

couplings, radio dials,
faces of old girl-friends.

My fingers lie like five
jetties that protect this shore

from the Great Lake's seven-
year rise and fall;

my hands teach: Our scarring
was not useful. Open. Take.

Last Summer

§ Always take advice.

I sit at the black table
with the white top, my back
to the screen door;

next to a tin ashtray
a cup of coffee cools.
I am opening my mail

this summer afternoon
(in swimming trunks,
sandals, a cigarette

in my mouth), reading,
as if fiction, how much
I owe, to whom I owe it,

and what for. One small
envelope I open last,
hold it to the light,

and shake the contents
down to one end ripped
through the stamp.

The paper is thin and blue,
and someone has printed
neatly, though not a woman:

"From over the water.
Minutes away. Now nearer.
Simply do not move."

I wait through summer
While birds chatter
near water. Do not move.

For a Wound

§ Skidding on her nails
across the chipped, split shale
rising from the water
to the parked car that kept
our warmth, the bitch clicked
after pipers skittering in shallows,

ran circles around us in the sand,
snapped at waves crashing
and spitting to drive her back.
She danced under a lowering sky,
clouds scudding toward the heavy forests,
lugging to the Pole.

We walked the hard dark beaches
of Lake Michigan, beneath
steep bluffs falling
from the edge of the city,
talking little, dull
from months of sending letters

across this gray lake, hesitant
and separating. For something to say
I whistled into the wind, whirling
the dog to her haunches; she skimmed
a partly buried log, fell hard,
yipped, whimpered to our feet:

blood told she'd ripped a nipple
from its neat black row. Now that scar
is old, white, hard; we walk
the frozen beaches held by blood.

These Are the Days

§ These are the dog days of August
and marriages. Here on the New Jersey farms

the drought is four years long,
the springs have dried, and rivers

like the Delaware show bare shale
and clog with trash. The leaves of corn

roll up and down again at night
like window shades. Undressing for bed

in silence and the dark the breeze
seems cooler. Outside the old dogs

grumble under the bushes as false thunder
rolls. A touch beneath the damp sheet

rumbles desire, insistent as a dog's bark.
In obligation to the moon,

huge, slow, red, and ominous,
we hold each other tightly in the heat

and dark, finding exhaustion
an unexpected spur to passion,

then turn back to waiting,
in the dark, for the weather

we had thought to break, this way.
The old dogs growl down to sleep.

On Not Wanting to Go on Vacation

§ I lash the luggage to the car top,
fill the tank, check maps,
drive off into the interior.
Everything is west from here.

I meet those who are coming back.
They have tales to tell of the back
country, how my hometown waits
for me, how the people all sit

on their front porches, watching
the car lights sweep by, wishing
the next car in the quiet street
were mine, with a desperate

love and disappointment mixed.
Outside Toledo I stop to fix
a tire. Bear on. Long years
ago we started out, with fear

in our hands at the reins, wet
leather staining our palms as we hit
the backs of the thin horses. Now
a Volkswagon pulls us around Chicago

with my hands stiff on the wheel.
In the back seat the baby wails
with her own memories of such sad
expeditions. We are following dead

ancestors home. Exploration
is never easy, for the sun
is always in one's eyes. Pulling up
to the curb, I let my hands drop

from the wheel, prepare to greet
old survivors in familiar streets.
Everything from here is east.
Bear up, old guest. Resist, resist.

Here There Is No Place

§ Here there is no place to grip;
all Wisconsin is fat country-side
in summer, stupid as butter.

Always a buzzing in the grass.

Everyone does his work.
The farms settle like cows,
rows of corn rattle slow tails.

Over the green ponds the flies sing.

Each small town dreaming
of a court-house, a radio station
above the bank.

Children calling on empty school-grounds.

Returning from the eastern cities,
the veins on the backs of my hands
bulge as I crush the map.

In my mind a low desperate hum.

In Father's Barn

§ 1.

In father's barn we stored old lumber
in 1944, filled with nails and knotholes,
rough, threatening our enemy overseas;

a national resource, my father thought,
like Victory Gardens my mother
planted, naming vegetables in Dutch

under her breath, careful to say
their English names outloud. In father's barn
his bicycle leaned each night against

the woodpile; to save gas he pedalled
off each morning with his lunchpail
to defend us all on overtime that year.

Mother saved fat in cans, angry
and blushing at the butcher's joke. I played
all through the war, burned my hand

melting tar in leaf fires, ran nails into
my feet climbing old wood stacked for a fort;
falling off the bicycle at dusk

I split my chin against the curb.
Bandaged against scars on the homefront,
I wept in father's barn, hoping to survive.

2.

I was seven then—to show her now
what I had stored in father's barn those
lean years, I took my daughter two decades

home; her seven years were fat,
she could not understand. Father is old wood,
knotted and dry, with a nail in his hip;

mother is a garden, pale flower, poor soil—
like children, they cannot understand
new Asian wars, burning jungle leaves.

Father, mother, daughter, all years
are war years until we can defend
our enemies at home. I cannot weep

now for myself, or you, my children,
dying, quick, unborn. In father's barn
at dusk I learn we shall survive.

III

Spring in Washington

§ The tourists arrive, swarming
over monuments, snapping Japanese
cameras on the Mall. Spring
leaps from the Potomac with the shad,
spawning in tidal pools and back runs.
Swamp crocus split, crack
open the dry sack of winter.

On the Hill Congressmen bloom,
April flowers in their lapels,
randy among the pert girls.
Paint gleams on the White House,
vacuousness grins among Senators.
A conference of dogwood convenes,
scenting the heavy air at State.

Mimosa and cherry blossom force
open the heart of the capital
of the free world, find frivolousness
green in the breasts of clerks.
All flags, initials, signatures
lose force, as the republic accepts
the *coup d'etat* of spring.

The President's Ghost Looks In

§ He fades slowly through the darkness
and fog of Washington; it is late in the year
and the rain mists his glasses—his vision
of the Capitol is streaming, is streaming.

Long black cars softly crush
through wet leaves in the gutters;
a cortege of trees creeps down the street
and all the flags are down, are down.

The inauguration stands stand skeletal,
the marble steps are nailed over with wood.
There will be no President next year,
no government, no news—there will be, will be

more long heavy days of rain and mist
through which the civil servants slouch
to bus-stops and muddy parking lots.
Some empty madness will set in, set in.

He stands beneath Ulysses Grant's
slouch hat and hunched shoulders; horses
begin to step slowly, stumble, through his mind.
America sets in; when it dies, it dies

easily, he thinks. Turning down the Mall,
he splashes past the temporary buildings,
hears mice in the dusty halls of agencies,
departments and commissions. I've had it, had it,

he whispers, I will go back away somewhere.
At the corner where the Park Police
mount their horses from a stump, he finds
a broken mirror on the walk, looks in, looks in.

Accident on Independence Avenue

§ The taxi hit her, and as she lay
with her cheek against the curb,
her shoes and skirt soaking up the snow,
she watched it skid, wheels locked,
and hit the parked Ford, chunks
of black ice falling from all the fenders,
until the pain hit her where she lay.

She blacked out, and then came back,
the waves of pain washing her up
and down again in the gutter slush,
until she did not know she screamed
or that she finally stopped. Her coat
was torn and wet, her jewelry like ice.
Someone gently turned her on her back.

She did not know they picked her up
and slid her in the ambulance, its siren
winding down around her and then up
and up, and she woke to whisper
to the frightened intern, that shit,
that shit, and fought for her handbag.
The morphine in the needle filled her up

with cotton, dust, uneasy sleep.
She remembered the Negro orderly
tucking her in her pain, and sometime
later felt her leg and hip were cut
and stitched again. That night she held
her own arms down while a red light
blinked, and she limped in and out of sleep.

Radio Soul

Now I will do nothing but listen.

—Walt Whitman,
Song of Myself

Everyone in America
is talking at once
about everything at once,

like a disc jockey
on a Negro station.
I hear some of what

is trying to be said
here and there
across the land,

listening tonight
to rock and roll,
and Freedom News

every fifteen minutes.
Everything on this radio
is black: Radio Soul

in the Soul Society.
My radio is white
on a white tabletop;

there's ah so much
pain in me, we sing
together—outside snow

is falling, millions
of words whispered over
and over on the air.

Black and White Together

§ I feel my way along the blackness
of the White House fence, against snow,
stroking its curlicues and points,
until I regain my wind. Silhouetted
in the glare of television lights,
the motorcycle cop stands in snow—
his boots, pistol, nightstick,
belts and helmet define limits
to the circling of the demonstrators
singing in the slow fall of snow—the white!

the black! These confrontations
frighten me. I fear concepts: power,
love, my hate, my weakness, black leather
in the snow, black fence circling
the White House. Staggering on flat
feet like a cop's, I aim dry
retchings at the national grass,
stroking the curlicues of my mind,
while High School Friends of SNCC
urge freedom songs and coffee, action
for despair—they puzzle over me,
an old man of thirty, struggling in the wind.

Stroking their nightsticks, the police
brace for cameras, adjust foul-weather
gear, and scowl for the late late news
direct from Pennsylvania Avenue.
The President sleeps through chants
of Freedom, Freedom, Freedom.
I know I do not understand, yet I sing
my songs for civil rights;
I wanted to be free for once. When
the cops moved in, it was on me, falling
in the white snow falling on the black snow.

All Clear

§ Lunch today was a double
gin gimlet with the double
divorcee from the office;

the newsboys wave the news
about Pleiku today
outside the restaurant,

the jets trail high
over the Potomac.
The rooms fill

with brass joking,
a waitress or two gets
the good word.

A sudden Caravelle
leaps above the gulls
gunning the wharves,

startles us all,
tips a tray from the arm
of a Negro busboy

who wipes up
looking up with white eyes.
Eating rice and fish

I swallow hard
while the sun breaks
bottles all over the room.

Her face is slightly
oriental when she smiles
All Clear over Washington.

Rest Stop in Raleigh

§ Midnight, and our Trailways
bus has stopped its long
degenerative whine

through Virginia, under stars
like winter cotton bolls.
We regroup from public bathrooms,

snack bars and candy racks,
pockets stuffed with Hersheys
and chewing gum; hang around

in clouds of gasoline and rubber,
wearing sunglasses.
The old Negroes from Newark

tote bundles of cardboard
tied with rope; the sailors
ache for coeds in kneesocks.

One disbelieves the South,
going into it—no stars
fall, no Carolina

moon tonight. One learns
January comes this far.
I do not want to go on.

At the water fountain I fill
my mouth, throw my head back,
gulp Seconal, and go on.

On the Town: New Orleans

§ The music along Bourbon rattled
the dry palms; we wet our whistles
on Jax Beer and joined in.

Everyone in the street made music;
the strippers taught us how.
Soon the street rocked,

iron twisted off the balconies
to take root and bloom
like giant flowers: red, gold,

blue, violet. Some climbed
the stems to heaven or wherever
it was Papa John fell into

by accidents within his heart.
Later, over coffee at Cafe du Monde,
while river smells misted

the trolley windows, the girls
seemed less vicious. The taxi back
to the hotel smelled of licorice.

The Summons

§ I have been preparing for California,
here in an eastern city,
with the January sun hazing the windows,
the dark trees clacking

and chirping in the gray wind.
I don't know yet if I must go,
but it is best to be prepared.
Also, there are many signs.

On the radio the Beatles shout
Hello Sunshine, and I am peeling
an orange on a blue plate.
My daughter is learning to thread

needles, a skill needed in California.
I am getting my fishing gear
in shape, oiling my hiking boots,
squinting up the barrels of the shotgun.

In the kitchen thick soup steams.
While the telephone goes on ringing
and ringing, my wife answers—
she is lovely, coming to tell me

the news about myself.
"They ask about you, in California."
"I know—I'll have to go soon."
"And us?" "I'll let you know."

She goes out of the room
with my daughter, picking her way
through ammunition, rags,
old magazines, my indecision.

She is going away from me east.
I know if I leave this house
it will shrink in on itself, the furnace
will shake late at night;

under the dark snow, the grass
will weep, the garbage cans roll
away down the cobbled alley.
How does one know what to care about?

The sun is fading toward California;
I reach out to feel its last rays
on the cold window. I reach across
the continent, my hand touches California.

Tauxemont Afternoon

for the Surovells

§ In that branch of religion which regards the
moralities of life, and the duties of a social being,
which teaches us to love our neighbors as ourselves, and to do good to all men, I am sure that
you and I do not differ.

—Thomas Jefferson, to Ezra Stiles,
June 25, 1819, Monticello

I

We gather here at Tauxemont
for warmth; together with wide
split-cane rakes on this half-acre
of Virginia's commonwealth,
in blue jeans, old Army shirts,
we hoard this wealth that grew
on trees, or bushes—sharing
bourbon from a bottle on the stump,
naming trees and bushes,
or their leaves: willow oak,
birch, magnolia, chestnut,
hickory, red maple, walnut—

here leaves are raked five times
each fall for compost; heaped up,
carried off in baskets, stuffed
into the chicken-wire bin
staked out behind the shed,
they draw red, gold, bright yellow,
black, magenta from the far November
sun. The fires of decomposition
burn deep—plunge your arm into
these millions and feel heat!

II

Virginia, you are the graveyard
of Presidents—down these roads
the Presidents have walked, and now
are buried beneath our feet:
from the first to next-to-last.
The pale light flickers on a hillside
in Arlington; the cut-glass chandeliers
at Mount Vernon stir in empty rooms.
Some burn their leaves in Tauxemont
and from the hill we see smoke
flow into the hollows between
the cheap tract houses—the smoke
like history in our lungs and eyes.

And this America of millions—
is there any warmth among us? Massed
together in the rising wind, we wait
dark storms closing from December
and the cold Atlantic, while west of here
our history evades us, smoking
across the Pacific to disappear
in Asian jungles, among exotic leaves,
new territories. Cheated by coasts,
we extend our search for violent identities
elsewhere, as our cities die around us—
we are breaking down under this slow
chemistry to smoke and ash
drifting across the land toward winter,
the last few months of a dark year.

III

... is it possible to have a small circle of friends,
friends of grace and purpose . . . on a basis of
mutual respect, work, and a kind of humorous,
informal dignity, in the United States?

—Clancy Sigal,
Going Away

Know your friends! Keep them close
for warmth, calm in the maelstrom from
across the Potomac outward everywhere.
We rest now, in this half-acre backyard
beneath dark trees, near brittle plants:
centered, in this eye that sees friends
close. Sharing bourbon and good cheese,
we sprawl in chairs left out from
the Fourth—our celebration of the death
of Jefferson—to catch the final sun,
and watch the dark clouds heap up east
of here. A chilling wind is rising
from the land, cold through our shirts,
bringing the last leaves down, to lie
unraked till spring. We end our day,
gathering rakes and sweaters from the lawn,
stacking baskets by the shed—

a small circle, we make jokes inside
around the fire, where pine twigs snap
and blaze between the silences of Bach;
ice cracks and melts in glasses
on the hearth. We do not differ
in the worship of this warmth.
Night cold begins to settle in the eaves.
Each hour the dark settles the plains,
the mountains, the far white beaches,
and for America the sun goes out.
Leaves scratch along the road through
shadows that are trees or Presidents;
last fires smoke red below us, to the west.

The Jar

§ The sky is low, gray;
an inversion holding
slow air and smoke
over the city. Now April,

and in this room
dullness also prevails;
all color's drawn

to one jar, thrown
on a stranger's wheel,
glazed earth red,
orange, a warm brown

burning inside.
I have been promised
help, despite myself,

and have seen
in the depth of glaze
all I lack—not of color
but of depth—

creator, there are many
flaws. I cross the room,
to touch orange, centering.

COLOPHON

The poems in this book are set in Baskerville types. The Linotype cutting used here is the most faithful to the original eighteenth-century version, and was produced from a complete font cast from the original matrices found at Paris in 1929. The display is set in Optima, a type face designed by Hermann Zapf for the Stempel Type Foundry.

The printing is directly from the type by Heritage Printers, Inc., on 60 lb. Warren's Olde Style white antique wove paper. The binding materials are by Columbia.

The design that appears on the title page and the binding was taken in part from an ancient alchemist's sign for water.

The book was designed by Gary Gore.

Pitt Poetry Series

James Den Boer, *Learning the Way*
Jon Anderson, *Looking for Jonathan*